What Do You Make?

A book for and about teachers

By Tom Hierck

Illustrations by Anne DeGrace

To my wife Ingrid and three children Kristin, David, and Shannon.
Thanks for your continued inspiration and support.
You remind me why teachers make a difference.

Library and Archives Canada Cataloguing in Publication

Hierck, Tom, 1960-
      What do you make? : a book for and about teachers / Tom
Hierck ; illustrator, Anne DeGrace.

ISBN 0-9736007-0-5

      1. Teachers--Pictorial works. I. DeGrace, Anne II. Title.

LB1033.H522 2004   371.1'022'2   C2004-904027-8

Printed in Canada.

The dinner guests were seated around a table discussing
public education. One man, a CEO, decided to explain the problem.

"What's a kid going to learn," he argued, "from someone who decided the best option in life was to become a teacher?"

"You're a teacher, Kristin," he said. "Be honest. What do you make?"

"You want to know what I make?"

"I make kids work harder than they ever thought they could."

"I can make a C+ feel like an Olympic gold medal
for the student who gave it everything...

...and an A⁻ feel like a knot in the stomach if the effort
wasn't the very best it could be."

"I make kids apologize, because they know it's the right thing to do."

"I make them write. I make them read, read, read."

"I can make parents tremble in fear when I call home...

…and then revel in the joy of the message I've shared about their child's accomplishment."

"You want to know what I make? I make kids wonder."

"I make them question. I make them criticize with a view towards improving a situation."

"I can make kids sit through 40 minutes of study hall...

...in absolute silence."

"I make them show all of their work in math...

...and hide it all on the final draft of their English essay."

"I immerse them in music and art and the joy of performance...

...so their lives are rich, full of kindness and culture,
and they take pride in themselves."

"I make them spell 'believe' and 'success' over and over again...

...until they will never misspell either one of those words again."

"I make them understand that if you have the brains (and they all do)...

...then follow your heart."

"And if anyone ever tries to judge you by what you make...

...you pay them no attention."

"You want to know what I make?"

"I'm a teacher, and I make a difference."

What Teachers Make

(or, If Things Don't Work Out, You Can Always Go to Law School)
by Taylor Mali

He says the problem with teachers is
What's a kid going to learn
from someone who decided his best option in life
was to become a teacher?
He reminds the other dinner guests that it's true
what they say about teachers:
Those who can, do; those who can't, teach.

I decide to bite my tongue instead of his
and resist the temptation to remind the dinner guests
that it's also true what they say about lawyers.

Because we're eating, after all, and this is polite company.

I mean, you're a teacher, Taylor.
Be honest. What do you make?

And I wish he hadn't done that
(asked me to be honest),
because, you see, I have a policy
about honesty and ass-kicking:
if you ask for it, then I have to let you have it.

You want to know what I make?

I make kids work harder than they ever thought they could.
I can make a C+ feel like a Congressional Medal of Honor
and an A- feel like a slap in the face.
How dare you waste my time
with anything less than your very best.

I make kids sit through 40 minutes of study hall
in absolute silence. No, you may not work in groups.

No, you may not ask a question.
Why won't I let you get a drink of water?
Because you're not thirsty, you're bored, that's why.
I make parents tremble in fear when I call home:
Hi. This is Mr. Mali. I hope I haven't called at a bad time,
I just wanted to talk to you about something your son said today.
He said, Leave the kid alone. I still cry sometimes, don't you?
And it was noblest act of courage I have ever seen.

I make parents see their children for who they are
and what they can be.

You want to know what I make?

I make kids wonder,
I make them question.
I make them criticize.
I make them apologize and mean it.
I make them write.
I make them read, read, read.
I make them spell definitely beautiful, definitely beautiful,
definitely beautiful
over and over and over again until they will never misspell
either one of those words again.
I make them show all their work in math
and hide it on their final drafts in English.
I make them understand that if you've got this,
then you follow this,
and if someone ever tries to judge you
by what you make, you give them this.

Let me break it down for you, so you know what I say is true:
I make a goddamn difference! What about you?

Author's Note

Teachers offer the greatest hope for our future. It is the one profession where passion and commitment reap major benefits. Teachers do make a difference. Every child that enters every classroom in September will be different in June. How they change rests, in part, with the experience they have during the year.
If the only objective is to get one year older, then little is required from the adults. Fortunately, more is expected and delivered.
Teaching is not a random act. All of the components of teaching, from the planning and preparation through to the modeling and mentoring, are designed to have an impact on each student.
While this design is critical, the most important criterion is our personal interactions and relationships with kids. I hope this book continues to inspire teachers and remind them of the connection they make to kids and how important this connection is. Every student needs a significant adult in school. As teachers we have the best opportunity to fill this role.